HOW LONG IS THE WATER CYCLE?

BY EMILY HUDD

CONTENT CONSULTANT

Craig R. Ferguson, PhD, Research Associate,
Atmospheric Sciences Research Center,
University at Albany

CAPSTONE PRESS
a capstone imprint

Fact Finders Books are published by Capstone Press,
1710 Roe Crest Drive, North Mankato, Minnesota 56003
www.mycapstone.com

Library of Congress Cataloging-in-Publication Data
Names: Hudd, Emily, author.
Title: How long is the water cycle? / by Emily Hudd.
Description: North Mankato, Minnesota : Capstone Press, [2020] | Series: How
  long does it take? | Audience: Grades 4 to 6. | Includes bibliographical
  references and index.
Identifiers: LCCN 2018061101 (print) | LCCN 2019003472 (ebook) | ISBN
  9781543573008 (ebook) | ISBN 9781543572940 (hardcover) | ISBN
  9781543575439 (pbk.)
Subjects: LCSH: Hydrologic cycle--Juvenile literature. | Hydrology--Juvenile
  literature.
Classification: LCC GB848 (ebook) | LCC GB848 .H8375 2020 (print) | DDC
  551.48--dc23
LC record available at https://lccn.loc.gov/2018061101

All internet sites appearing in back matter were available and accurate when this book was sent to press.

Editorial Credits
Editor: Marie Pearson
Designer and production specialist: Dan Peluso

Photo Credits
iStockphoto: eddieberman, 11; NASA: JSC, 14; Science Source: Power and Syred, 9; Shutterstock Images: Abramov Timur, 21, Artisticco, 7, Creative Travel Projects, 18, Kateryna Mashkevych, 12–13, KC Lens and Footage, cover (clouds), kristof lauwers, 22, Lukas Kastner, cover (water), michelmond, 24, saiko3p, 28, Sanchik, 5, Sharon Morris, 17, Tropical studio, 27

Design Elements: Red Line Editorial

TABLE OF CONTENTS

RAINY DAY

A boy hurries to the creek. It rained last night. The stream will be high enough to sail a paper boat. He places the boat in the water. The current carries it away. The boy follows it as it winds through the woods. Then the stream widens. It pushes the boat into a lake. The boy watches the boat disappear.

The water cycle refers to water's movement and storage on Earth. The cycle does not have a beginning or end. It happens in the hydrosphere. The hydrosphere is made of all the water on Earth.

It includes water in the air, on the surface, and underground. The water cycle began when Earth formed 4.5 billion years ago. And it continues today!

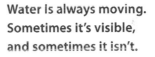

Water is always moving. Sometimes it's visible, and sometimes it isn't.

CHAPTER ONE

EVAPORATION

Water moving from Earth's surface to the air is one part of the water cycle. The main way that happens is evaporation. Evaporation happens when water changes from a liquid into a gas or **vapor**. Heat and wind help evaporation. The sun heats Earth's surface. As the temperature changes, winds blow across the ground. At the same time, heat from the sun warms water on Earth. Evaporation requires energy. That energy comes from the sun's heat and the wind. Energy makes water **molecules** spread farther apart. The water changes from a liquid to a gas or vapor. It rises into the air.

vapor—a gas made from something that is usually a liquid or solid at normal temperatures

molecule—the smallest physical unit of an element

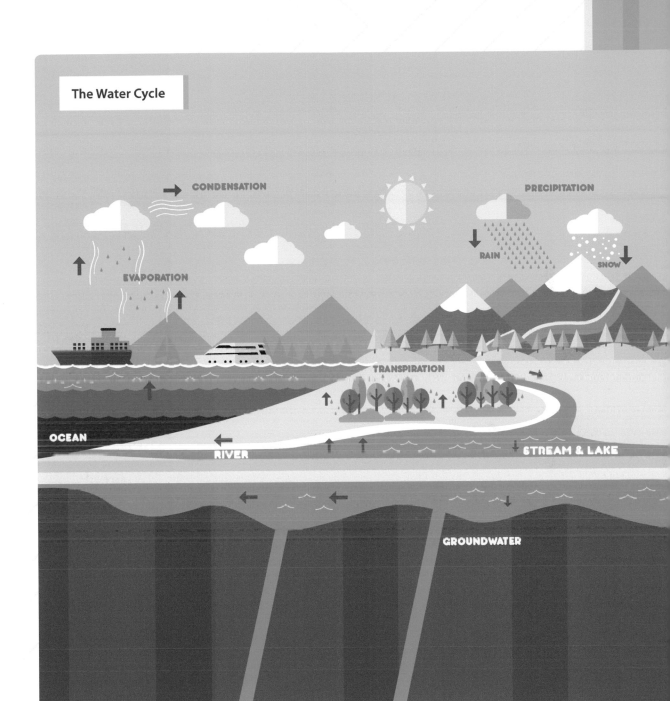

The Water Cycle

CONDENSATION

PRECIPITATION

EVAPORATION

RAIN

SNOW

TRANSPIRATION

OCEAN

RIVER

STREAM & LAKE

GROUNDWATER

Evaporation is an important part of the water cycle. Most water in the **atmosphere** comes from evaporated ocean water. Only 10 percent comes from transpiration on land. Transpiration happens when water stored in plants returns to the atmosphere. Water evaporates from inside the leaves as they use sunlight to make food. The amount of water plants transpire depends on the **climate** and plant. Usually plants in tropical climates transpire more than those in other climates. Tropical climates have longer growing seasons. Water is more available.

FACT
People use evaporation to harvest salt. They flood shallow ponds with ocean salt water. Heat from sunlight makes the water evaporate. Salt is left behind.

atmosphere—the layers of air that surround Earth
climate— the temperature, weather, and environment of a certain area

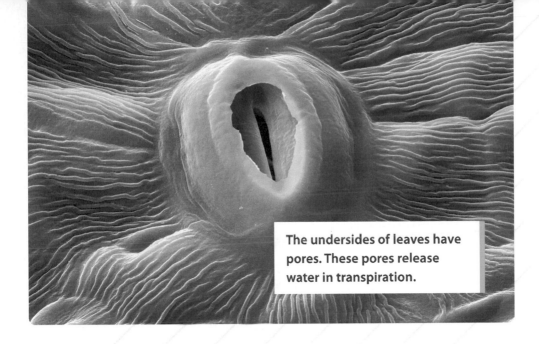

The undersides of leaves have pores. These pores release water in transpiration.

The least common way for water to return to the atmosphere is sublimation. Sublimation is when ice turns right into gas. It skips the liquid phase. Sublimation happens in the Rocky Mountains in late winter and early spring. Warm, dry winds raise the temperature quickly as they travel down the eastern sides of the mountains. The warm air hits the cold snow on the mountains. The snow becomes water vapor.

CHAPTER TWO

CONDENSATION

Condensation is the next stage in the water cycle. It is when water vapor in the air changes into liquid. As water vapor rises in the air, the molecules are spread out. They cool as they go higher. This causes the molecules to condense. They come close together. Typically, water vapor condenses

FACT

Condensation is the opposite of evaporation.

on tiny bits of dust, sea salt, and soot in the air. This process creates liquid water droplets. A large collection of droplets form a cloud. People can't see water droplets in the air. But they can see clouds.

Condensation can be seen on a cold beverage cup on a hot day. The cold drink causes water vapor in the air to condense on the cup.

Altocumulus clouds are often found in groups.

Different types of clouds form at different heights in the sky. Fog is a type of cloud that touches the ground. Low-level nimbostratus clouds are less than 6,500 feet (2,000 meters) from the ground. They are usually dark and thick. Flat altostratus and puffy altocumulus clouds form between 6,500 feet (2,000 m) and 20,000 feet (6,000 m). Airplanes fly as high as 39,600 feet (12,000 m).

Clouds give clues about the weather to come. Altocumulus clouds can be a warning that a storm is coming. High-level cirrus clouds are more than 20,000 feet (6,000 m) above the ground. They are usually made of ice, so they don't produce rain. They look thin and wispy. These clouds are normally a sign of calm weather.

FACT Over the ocean, clouds are more common in the morning. Over land, they are more common in the evening.

Cumulonimbus storm clouds form high above other clouds.

Fair weather cumulus clouds and cumulonimbus storm clouds are tall. Cumulonimbus cloud tops can reach heights of more than 50,000 feet (15,000 m). Warm, upward winds form them. As the winds rise, the air gets cooler.

HOW DO CLOUDS FLOAT?

Clouds are made of liquid water. The weight of a cloud depends on how much water it holds. Storm clouds often have larger water droplets than other clouds. Scientists think an average storm cloud could have 220 tons (200 metric tons) of water. That much water weighs a bit more than 14 school buses! Clouds float because the particles are too small to fall. It is similar to how dust appears to float when spotted in a sunbeam coming through a window.

Moisture in the winds condenses into droplets. The condensation releases energy. The energy warms the air, causing the cloud to rise and form more droplets. The energy from the clouds and wind can produce lightning, strong winds, and rain.

Strong winds move clouds around Earth until the next stage of the water cycle. Most water spends about nine days in the atmosphere before falling back to the surface.

CHAPTER THREE

PRECIPITATION

Water leaves the atmosphere to continue the water cycle. It falls out of clouds in a process called precipitation. Precipitation is an important part of the water cycle. It provides fresh water to Earth's surface. All living things on Earth need water to survive. Some plants in the desert can live with little water. Some animals live completely in water. But all plants and animals need some amount of water. Different parts of the world get different amounts of precipitation.

Rain is the most common form of precipitation. Raindrops form when many water droplets **collide**. On their own, droplets are too small to fall.

collide—to bump into another

They are tiny. The upward wind that pushes up the cloud

is stronger than the **gravity** pulling the droplets toward the ground.

It takes millions of cloud droplets to make one raindrop. They condense and stick together when they collide. When the raindrop is big enough, gravity pulls it to the ground.

Precipitation provides living things with some of the water they need to survive.

gravity—a force that pulls objects with mass together; gravity pulls objects down toward the center of Earth

Snow may stay frozen for months before it melts and soaks into the ground.

Snow and hail are other forms of precipitation. They are frozen water droplets. Water freezes at temperatures below 32 degrees Fahrenheit (0 degrees Celsius). This is called the freezing point of water. Except in tropical climates, most raindrops start off above as snowflakes. The snow melts into rain as it falls through air above the freezing point.

By the time the raindrops reach the ground, they are liquid. When the air is very warm and dry, the raindrops may evaporate before reaching the surface. In other places, the surface temperatures are below freezing. Snow stays frozen. It collects on the ground. When the temperature warms, it melts into liquid water that plants and animals can use.

Hailstones are ice chunks that form during thunderstorms. Snowflakes fall to the bottom of the storm clouds and rise again to the top one or more times. With each trip, another layer of ice is added, and the hail grows in size. Hail can damage cars, houses, and crops.

FACT

The largest piece of hail recorded in the United States fell in 2010. It was 8 inches (20 cm) wide. It weighed almost 2 pounds (0.9 kilograms).

CHAPTER FOUR

INFILTRATION AND RUNOFF

Precipitation can interact with the ground in two ways. It may soak into the soil. This process is called infiltration. Or it may run along the surface into a stream, river, or body of water. This water is called runoff. Infiltration and runoff are important parts of the water cycle. They provide plants, animals, and humans with the water they need to survive. Most water is used for growing crops and livestock. People also drink some water.

Storm drains collect runoff water to prevent dangerous flooding. The water is carried to either a facility where it is cleaned or a body of water.

The amount of time it takes for water to cycle back to the atmosphere varies. It depends on where the water falls.

Leaves can slow rain's descent. This reduces runoff.

If it falls on the ocean, it could evaporate in a few days. If it falls on soil, it could be **absorbed**. It might go deep into the ground. After many years, it could end up at the bottom of a lake.

The type of soil determines how deep water will go. Water drains quickly through sand. It travels easily around and between the tiny grains. Clay is dense. It is difficult for water to pass through.

Forests have many trees and leaves hanging over the ground. Water might fall on the leaves and slowly drip to the ground days or weeks after it falls. This allows more water to soak into the ground over time. It creates less runoff than areas with no trees or plants.

absorb—to take in water

Extreme cases of runoff include flooding.

After water is absorbed, it moves through soil. It carries nutrients from one place to another. Water usually stays in the soil from two weeks to one year. Then it moves on to another part of the water cycle. If water seeps as deep as the **water table**, it could remain there for as long as 10,000 years!

water table—a layer underground, below which the soil and rock is always soaked with water; it is tapped for drinking water through wells and springs

If the soil is frozen or already wet, water that falls on it might not be absorbed. The water sits on top of the soil. It becomes runoff water and flows across the ground. Sometimes sewers carry runoff under the street.

Gravity affects the flow of runoff. It pulls water down along Earth's surface. The **slope** of land determines the speed of flowing water. Runoff can be powerful. Flowing water can break down rocks. This process is called erosion. It can change the shape of land over time. Runoff is one of the main ways water travels across Earth's surface.

FACT Part of the reason oceans are salty is from runoff. Salt in soil has been carried with runoff water to the ocean.

slope—the upward or downward tilt of a piece of land

CHAPTER FIVE

COLLECTION AND STORAGE

Runoff and groundwater may end up in rivers and streams. They carry the water to larger bodies of water such as ponds, lakes, and the ocean. It can take a few days or several months for water to move from a river to a larger body of water. Or, during precipitation, water may skip the infiltration and runoff stage. It can fall directly into a lake or ocean. It moves to the next stage of the water cycle. This stage is storage.

FACT

Oceans cover 71 percent of Earth's surface.

The ocean stores vast amounts of water.

Bodies of water store water. Water is also stored in the atmosphere as vapor. It is stored as liquid in underground **aquifers**. It is stored for different amounts of time depending on the location.

aquifer—a natural rock formation underground that collects and stores water

Cold temperatures can keep water stored as ice for a long time. Glaciers are layers of snow that have turned into ice over time. A water droplet can be frozen and stored in a glacier for millions of years.

Water deep within a glacier can stay there for a very long time.

GROUNDWATER STORAGE

Some water is stored underground. After infiltration, it goes deep into the soil. It can be stored in an aquifer. An aquifer is a layer of rock that holds water. The rock has openings where water can pass through or be stored. This is where water from wells comes from. Some wells are drilled hundreds or thousands of feet deep to reach the aquifer.

The ocean holds about 96 percent of the water on Earth. Most water spends time in the ocean. Being in storage does not mean water stops moving. The ocean is never still. Currents always move the water around.

Storage is the stage where water can spend the most time. One drop of water can spend more than 3,000 years in the ocean. It can spend 10,000 years in an aquifer before it reaches the surface and evaporates. Then the water cycle continues!

GLOSSARY

absorb (ub-ZORB)—to take in water

aquifer (AH-kwi-fer)—a natural rock formation underground that collects and stores water

atmosphere (AT-muhs-feer)—the layers of air that surround Earth

climate (KLYE-mit)—the temperature, weather, and environment of a certain area

collide (kuh-LIDE)—to bump into another

gravity (GRAH-vih-tee)—a force that pulls objects with mass together; gravity pulls objects down toward the center of Earth

molecule (MAH-luh-kyool)—the smallest physical unit of an element

slope (SLOHP)—the upward or downward tilt of a piece of land

vapor (VAY-pur)—a gas made from something that is usually a liquid or solid at normal temperatures

water table (WAH-tur TAY-bul)—a layer underground, below which the soil and rock is always soaked with water; it is tapped for drinking water through wells and springs

ADDITIONAL RESOURCES

FURTHER READING

Enz, Tammy. *Liquid Planet: Exploring Water on Earth with Science Projects*. Discover Earth Science. North Mankato, Minn.: Capstone Press, 2016.

Olien, Rebecca. *The Water Cycle at Work*. Water in Our World. North Mankato, Minn.: Capstone Press, 2016.

Olien, Rebecca. *Water Sources*. Water in Our World. North Mankato, Minn.: Capstone Press, 2016.

Sharif-Draper, Maryam. *Earth*. DK Find Out! New York: DK/Penguin Random House, 2017.

CRITICAL THINKING QUESTIONS

1. Why are evaporation and condensation opposites?

2. In your own words, describe a water droplet traveling through each stage of the water cycle. Use evidence from the text to support your answer.

3. Each chapter talks about a different stage of the water cycle. For each stage, find one way it influences life on Earth.

INTERNET SITES

DK Find Out! Water Cycle
https://www.dkfindout.com/us/earth/water-cycle/

NASA Climate Kids: What is the Water Cycle?
https://climatekids.nasa.gov/water-cycle/

National Geographic Kids: The Water Cycle
https://www.natgeokids.com/uk/discover/science/nature/water-cycle/

INDEX

ABOUT THE AUTHOR

Emily Hudd is a full-time children's author who loves writing nonfiction on a variety of topics. She lives in Minnesota with her husband.